Oct 12th 1900.

Theo. Seminary

Virginia.

HUMILITY

THE BEAUTY OF HOLINESS

Lord Jesus ! may our Holiness be perfect Humility !
Let Thy perfect Humility be our Holiness !

BY

REV. ANDREW MURRAY

AUTHOR OF "ABIDE IN CHRIST," "LIKE CHRIST,"
"BE PERFECT," ETC.

NEW YORK   CHICAGO   TORONTO

Fleming H. Revell Company

Publishers of Evangelical Literature

PREFACE.

THERE are three great motives that urge us to humility. It becomes me as a creature, as a sinner, as a saint. The first we see in the heavenly hosts, in unfallen man, in Jesus as Son of Man. The second appeals to us in our fallen state, and points out the only way through which we can return to our right place as creatures. In the third we have the mystery of grace, which teaches us that, as we lose ourselves in the overwhelming greatness of redeeming love, humility becomes to us the consummation of everlasting blessedness and adoration.

In our ordinary religious teaching the second aspect has been too exclusively put in the foreground, so that some have even gone to the extreme of saying that we must keep sinning if we are indeed to keep humble. Others again have thought that the strength of self-condemnation is the secret of humility. And the Christian life has suffered loss, where believers have not been distinctly guided to see that, even in our relation as creatures, nothing is more natural and beautiful and blessed than to be nothing, that God may be all ; or, where it has not been made clear that it is not sin that humbles most, but grace, and that it is the soul, led through its sinfulness to be occupied with God in His wonderful glory as God, as Creator, and Redeemer, that will truly take the lowest place before Him.

In these meditations I have, for more than one reason, almost exclusively directed attention to the humility that becomes us as creatures. It is not only

that the connection between humility
and sin is so abundantly set forth in all
our religious teaching, but because I believe that for the fullness of the Christian
life it is indispensable that prominence
be given to the other aspect. If Jesus is
indeed to be our example in His lowliness, we need to understand the princi-
ples in which it was rooted, and in which
we find the common ground on which we
stand with Him, and in which our likeness to Him is to be attained. If we
are indeed to be humble, not only before God but towards men, if humility is
to be our joy, we must see that it is not
only the mark of shame because of sin, but,
apart from all sin, a being clothed upon
with the very beauty and blessedness of
heaven and of Jesus. We shall see that
just as Jesus found His glory in taking
the form of a servant, so when He said
to us, "Whosoever would be first among

you shall be your servant," He simply taught us the blessed truth that there is nothing so divine and heavenly as being the servant and helper of all. The faithful servant who recognizes his position finds a real pleasure in supplying the wants of the master or his guests. When we see that humility is something infinitely deeper than contrition, and accept it as our participation in the life of Jesus, we shall begin to learn that it is our true nobility, and that to prove it in being servants of all is the highest fulfillment of our destiny, as men created in the image of God.

When I look back upon my own religious experience, or round upon the Church of Christ in the world, I stand amazed at the thought of how little humility is sought after as the distinguishing feature of the discipleship of Jesus. In preaching and living, in the daily in-

tercourse of the home and social life, in
the more special fellowship with Christians, in the direction and performance
of work for Christ,—alas! how much
proof there is that humility is not esteemed the cardinal virtue, the only root
from which the graces can grow, the one
indispensable condition of true fellowship with Jesus. That it should have
been possible for men to say of those
who claim to be seeking the higher holiness, that the profession has not been
accompanied with increasing humility, is
a loud call to all earnest Christians, however much or little truth there be in the
charge, to prove that meekness and lowliness of heart are the chief mark by
which they who follow the meek and
lowly lamb of God are to be known.

CONTENTS.

1.

HUMILITY: THE GLORY OF THE CREATURE.

"They shall cast their crowns before the throne, saying: Worthy art Thou, our Lord and our God, to receive the glory and the honor and the power: for Thou didst create all things, and because of Thy will they were, and were created."—REV. iv. 11.

WHEN God created the universe, it was with the one object of making the creature partaker of His perfection and blessedness, and so showing forth in it the glory of His love and wisdom and power. God wished to reveal Himself in and through created beings by communicating to them as much of His own

goodness and glory as they were capable
of receiving. But this communication
was not a giving to the creature something which it could possess in itself, a
certain life or goodness, of which it had
the charge and disposal. By no means.
But as God is the ever-living, ever-pres-
ent, ever-acting One, who upholdeth all
things by the word of His power, and in
whom all things exist, the relation of the
creature to God could only be one of
unceasing, absolute, universal dependence. As truly as God by His power
once created, so truly by that same
power must God every moment maintain. The creature has not only to look
back to the origin and first beginning of
existence, and acknowledge that it there
owes everything to God ; its chief care,
its highest virtue, its only happiness, now
and through all eternity, is to present
itself an empty vessel, in which God can

dwell and manifest His power and goodness.

The life God bestows is imparted not once for all, but each moment continuously, by the unceasing operation of His mighty power. Humility, the place of entire dependence on God, is, from the very nature of things, the first duty and the highest virtue of the creature, and the root of every virtue.

And so pride, or the loss of this humility, is the root of every sin and evil. It was when the now fallen angels began to look upon themselves with self-complacency that they were led to disobedience, and were cast down from the light of heaven into outer darkness. Even so it was, when the serpent breathed the poison of his pride, the desire to be as God, into the hearts of our first parents, that they, too, fell from their high estate into all the wretchedness in which man is now sunk. In heaven and earth, pride, self-exaltation, is the gate and the birth, and the curse, of hell. (See Note A.)

Hence, it follows that nothing can be our redemption, but the restoration of the lost humility, the original and only true relation of the creature to its God. And so Jesus came to bring humility back to earth, to make us partakers of it, and by it to save us. In heaven He humbled Himself to become man. The humility we see in Him possessed Him in heaven ; it brought Him, he brought it, from there. Here on earth " He humbled Himself, and became obedient unto death"; His humility gave His death its value, and so became our redemption. And now the salvation He imparts is nothing less and nothing else than a communication of His own life and death, His own disposition and spirit,

His own humility, as the ground and root of His relation to God and His redeeming work. Jesus Christ took the place and fulfilled the destiny of man, as a creature, by His life of perfect humility. His humility is our salvation. His salvation is our humility.

And so the life of the saved ones, of the saints, must needs bear this stamp of deliverance from sin, and full restoration to their original state; their whole relation to God and man marked by an all-pervading humility. Without this there can be no true abiding in God's presence, or experience of His favor and the power of His spirit; without this no abiding faith, or love or joy or strength. Humility is the only soil in which the graces root; the lack of humility is the sufficient explanation of every defect and failure. Humility is not so much a grace or virtue along with others; it is the root of all, because it alone takes the right attitude before God, and allows Him as God to do all.

God has so constituted us as reasonable beings, that the truer the insight into the real nature or the absolute need of a command, the readier and fuller will be our obedience to it. The call to humility has been too little regarded in the Church, because its true nature and importance has been too little apprehended. It is not a something which we bring to God, or He bestows; it is simply *the sense of entire nothingness, which comes when we see how truly God is all, and in which we make way for God to be all.* When the creature realizes that this is the true nobility, and consents to be with his will, his mind, and his affections, the form, the vessel in which the life and glory of God are to work and manifest themselves, he sees that humility is simply acknowledging the truth of his position as creature, and yielding to God his place.

In the life of earnest Christians, of those who pursue and profess holiness, humility ought to be the chief mark of their uprightness. It is often said that it is not so. May not one reason be that in the teaching and example of the Church, it has never had that place of supreme importance which belongs to it? And that this, again, is owing to the neglect of this truth, that strong as sin is as a motive to humility, there is one of still wider and mightier influence, that which makes the angels, that which made Jesus, that which makes the holiest of saints in heaven, so humble; that the first and chief mark of the relation of the creature, the secret of his blessedness, is the humility and nothingness which leaves God free to be all?

I am sure there are many Christians

who will confess that their experience
has been very much like my own in this,
that we had long known the Lord without realizing that meekness and lowliness
of heart are to be the distinguishing feature of the disciple as they were of the
Master. And further, that this humility
is not a thing that will come of itself, but
that it must be made the object of special desire and prayer and faith and practice. As we study the word, we shall see
what very distinct and oft-repeated in-
structions Jesus gave His disciples on
this point, and how slow they were in
understanding Him. Let us, at the very
commencement of our meditations, ad-
mit that there is nothing so natural to
man, nothing so insidious and hidden
from our sight, nothing so difficult and
dangerous, as pride. Let us feel that
nothing but a very determined and per-
severing waiting on God and Christ will

discover how lacking we are in the grace
of humility, and how impotent to obtain
what we seek. Let us study the character of Christ until our souls are filled
with the love and admiration of His lowliness. And let us believe that, when we
are broken down under a sense of our
pride, and our impotence to cast it out,
Jesus Christ Himself will come in to im-
part this grace, too, as a part of His wondrous life within us.

II.

HUMILITY: THE SECRET OF REDEMPTION.

"Have this mind in you which was also in Christ Jesus: who emptied Himself, taking the form of a servant; and humbled Himself, becoming obedient even unto death. Wherefore God also highly exalted him."—PHIL. ii. 5-7.

No tree can grow except on the root from which it sprang. Through all its existence it can only live with the life that was in the seed that gave it being. The full apprehension of this truth in its application to the first and the Second Adam cannot but help us greatly to understand both the need and the nature of the redemption there is in Jesus.

The Need.—When the Old Serpent, he who had been cast out from heaven for his pride, whose whole nature as devil was pride, spoke his words of temptation into the ear of Eve, these words carried with them the very poison of hell. And when she listened, and yielded her desire and her will to the prospect of being as God, knowing good and evil, the poison entered into her soul and blood and life, destroying for ever that blessed humility and dependence upon God which would have been our everlasting happiness. And instead of this, her life and the life of the race that sprang from her became corrupted to its very root with that most terrible of all sins and all curses, the poison of Satan's own pride. All the wretchedness of which this world has been the scene, all its wars and bloodshed among the nations, all its selfishness and suffering, all its ambitions and jealousies, all its broken hearts and embittered lives, with all its daily unhappiness, have their origin in what this cursed, hellish pride, either our own, or that of others, has brought us. It is pride that made redemption needful; it is from our pride we need above everything to be redeemed. And our insight into the need of redemption will largely depend upon our knowledge of the terrible nature of the power that has entered our being.

No tree can grow except on the root from which it sprang. The power that Satan brought from hell, and cast into man's life, is working daily, hourly, with mighty power throughout the world. Men suffer from it; they fear and fight and flee it; and yet they know not whence it comes, whence it has its terrible supremacy. No wonder they do not know where or how it is to be overcome. Pride has its root and strength in a terrible spiritual power, outside of us as well as within us; as needful as it is that we confess and deplore it as our very own, is it to know it in its Satanic origin. If this leads us to utter despair of ever conquering or casting it out, it will lead us all the sooner to that supernatural power in which alone our deliverance is to be found—the redemption of the Lamb of God. The hopeless struggle against the workings of self and pride within us may indeed become still more hopeless as we think of the power of darkness behind it all; the utter despair will fit us the better for realizing and accepting a power and a life outside of ourselves too, even the humility of heaven as brought down and brought nigh by the Lamb of God, to cast out Satan and his pride.

No tree can grow except on the root from which it sprang. Even as we need to look to the first Adam and his fall to

know the power of the sin within us, we
need to know well the Second Adam and
His power to give within us a life of
humility as real and abiding and over-
mastering as has been that of pride. We
have our life from and in Christ, as truly,
yea more truly, than from and in Adam.
We are to walk "rooted in Him," "hold-
ing fast the Head from whom the whole
body increaseth with the increase of
God." The life of God which in the
incarnation entered human nature, is the
root in which we are to stand and grow;
it is the same almighty power that worked
there, and thence onward to the resurrection, which works daily in us. Our
one need is to study and know and trust
the life that has been revealed in Christ
as the life that is now ours, and waits for
our consent to gain possession and mas-
tery of our whole being.

In this view it is of inconceivable

importance that we should have right thoughts of what Christ is, of what really constitutes him the Christ, and specially of what may be counted His chief characteristic, the root and essence of all His character as our Redeemer. There can be but one answer: it is His humility. What is the incarnation but His heavenly humility, His emptying Himself and becoming man? What is His life on earth but humility; His taking the form of a servant? And what is His atonement but humility? "He humbled Himself and became obedient unto death." And what is His ascension and His glory, but humility exalted to the throne and crowned with glory? "He humbled Himself, therefore God highly exalted Him." In heaven, where He was with the Father, in His birth, in His life, in His death, in His sitting on the throne, it is all, it is nothing but humility. Christ is the humility of God embodied in human nature; the Eternal Love humbling itself, clothing itself in the garb of meekness and gentleness, to win and serve and save us. As the love and condescension of God makes Him the benefactor and helper and servant of all, so Jesus of necessity was the Incarnate Humility. And so He is still in the midst of the throne, the meek and lowly Lamb of God.

If this be the root of the tree, its nature must be seen in every branch and leaf and fruit. If humility be the first, the all-including grace of the life of Jesus,— if humility be the secret of His atonement,—then the health and strength of our spiritual life will entirely depend upon our putting this grace first too, and making humility the chief thing we admire in Him, the chief thing we ask of Him, the one thing for which we sacrifice all else.[1]

Is it any wonder that the Christian life is so often feeble and fruitless, when the very root of the Christ life is neglected, is unknown? Is it any wonder that the joy of salvation is so little felt, when that in which Christ found it and brings it is so little sought? Until a humility which will rest in nothing less than the end and death of self; which gives up all the honor of men as Jesus did, to seek the honor that comes from God alone; which absolutely makes and counts itself nothing, that God may be all, that the Lord alone may be exalted, — until such a humility be what we seek in Christ above our chief joy, and welcome at any price, there is very little hope of a religion that will conquer the world.

---

[1] See Note B.

I cannot too earnestly plead with my reader, if possibly his attention has never yet been specially directed to the want there is of humility within him or around him, to pause and ask whether he sees much of the spirit of the meek and lowly Lamb of God in those who are called by His name. Let him consider how all want of love, all indifference to the needs, the feelings, the weakness of others; all sharp and hasty judgments and utterances, so often excused under the plea of being outright and honest; all manifestations of temper and touchiness and irritation; all feelings of bitterness and estrangement,—have their root in nothing but pride, that ever seeks itself, and his eyes will be opened to see how a dark, shall I not say a devilish pride, creeps in almost everywhere, the assemblies of the saints not excepted. Let him begin to ask what would be the effect, if in himself and around him, if towards fellow-saints and the world, believers were really permanently guided by the humility of Jesus; and let him say if the cry of our whole heart, night and day, ought not to be, Oh for the humility of Jesus in myself and all around me! Let him honestly fix his heart on his own lack of the humility which has been revealed in the likeness of Christ's life, and in the whole character of His redemption, and he will begin to feel as if he had never yet really known what Christ and His salvation is.

Believer! *study the humility of Jesus.* This is the secret, the hidden root of thy redemption. Sink down into it deeper day by day. Believe with thy whole heart that this Christ, whom God has given thee, even as His divine humility wrought the work for thee, will enter in to dwell and work within thee too, and make thee what the Father would have thee be.

III.

THE HUMILITY OF JESUS.

" I am in the midst of you as he that serveth."
—Luke xxii. 26.

In the Gospel of John we have the
inner life of our Lord laid open to us.
Jesus speaks frequently of His relation
to the Father, of the motives by which
He is guided, of His consciousness of
the power and spirit in which He acts.
Though the word humble does not occur,
we shall nowhere in Scripture see so
clearly wherein His humility consisted.
We have already said that this grace is
in truth nothing but that simple consent
of the creature to let God be all, in virtue
of which it surrenders itself to His work-

(32)

ing alone. In Jesus we shall see how both as the Son of God in heaven, and as man upon earth, He took the place of entire subordination, and gave God the honor and the glory which is due to Him. And what He taught so often was made true to Himself: "He that humbleth himself shall be exalted." As it is written, "He humbled himself, therefore God highly exalted Him."

Listen to the words in which our Lord speaks of His relation to the Father, and see how unceasingly He uses the words *not*, and *nothing*, of Himself. The *not I*, in which Paul expresses his relation to Christ, is the very spirit of what Christ says of His relation to the Father.

"The Son can do *nothing* of Himself" (John v. 19).

"I can of My own self do *nothing;* My judgment is just, because I seek *not* Mine own will" (John v. 30).

"I receive *not* glory from men" (John v. 41).

"I am come *not* to do Mine own will" (John vi. 38).

"My teaching is *not* Mine" (John vii. 16).

"I am *not* come of Myself" (John vii. 28).

"I do *nothing* of Myself" (John viii. 28).

"I have *not* come of Myself, but He sent Me" (John viii. 42).

"I seek *not* Mine own glory" (John viii. 50).

"The words that I say, I speak *not* from Myself" (John xiv. 10).

"The word which ye hear is *not* Mine" (John xiv. 24).

These words open to us the deepest roots of Christ's life and work. They tell us how it was that the Almighty God was able to work His mighty redemption work through Him. They show what

Christ counted the state of heart which became Him as the Son of the Father. They teach us what the essential nature and life is of that redemption which Christ accomplished and now communicates. It is this: He was nothing, that God might be all. He resigned Himself with His will and His powers entirely for the Father to work in Him. Of His own power, His own will, and His own glory, of His whole mission with all His works and His teaching,—of all this He said, It is not I; I am nothing; I have given Myself to the Father to work; I am nothing, the Father is all.

This life of entire self-abnegation, of absolute submission and dependence upon the Father's will, Christ found to be one of perfect peace and joy. He lost nothing by giving all to God. God honored His trust, and did all for Him, and then exalted Him to His own right

hand in glory.   And because Christ had
thus humbled Himself before God, and
God was ever before Him, He found it
possible to humble Himself before men
too, and to be the Servant of all.   His
humility was simply the surrender of
Himself to God, to allow Him to do in
Him what He pleased, whatever men
around might say of Him, or do to Him.

It is in this state of mind, in this spirit
and disposition, that the redemption of
Christ has its virtue and efficacy.   It is
to bring us to this disposition that we
are made partakers of Christ.   This is
the true self-denial to which our Saviour
calls us, the acknowledgment that self
has nothing good in it, except as an
empty vessel which God must fill, and
that its claim to be or do anything may
not for a moment be allowed.   It is in
this, above and before everything, in
which the conformity to Jesus consists,

the being and doing nothing of ourselves,
that God may be all.

Here we have the root and nature of
true humility. It is because this is not
understood or sought after, that our humility is so superficial and so feeble. We
must learn of Jesus, how He is meek and
lowly of heart. He teaches us where
true humility takes its rise and finds its
strength—in the knowledge that it is God
who worketh all in all, that our place is
to yield to Him in perfect resignation
and dependence, in full consent to be
and to do nothing of ourselves. This is
the life Christ came to reveal and to im-
part—a life to God that came through
death to sin and self. If we feel that
this life is too high for us and beyond our
reach, it must but the more urge us to
seek it in Him; it is the indwelling Christ
who will live in us this life, meek and
lowly. If we long for this, let us, mean-

time, above everything, seek the holy
secret of the knowledge of the nature of
God, as He every moment works all in
all; the secret, of which all nature and
every creature, and above all, every child
of God, is to be the witness,—that it is
nothing but a vessel, a channel, through
which the living God can manifest the
riches of His wisdom, power, and goodness. The root of all virtue and grace,
of all faith and acceptable worship, is that
we know that we have nothing but what
we receive, and bow in deepest humility
to wait upon God for it.

It was because this humility was not
only a temporary sentiment, wakened up
and brought into exercise when He
thought of God, but the very spirit of
His whole life, that Jesus was just as
humble in His intercourse with men as
with God. He felt Himself the Servant
of God for the men whom God made and

loved; as a natural consequence, He counted Himself the Servant of men, that through Him God might do His work of love. He never for a moment thought of seeking His honor, or asserting His power to vindicate Himself. His whole spirit was that of a life yielded to God to work in. It is not until Christians study the humility of Jesus as the very essence of His redemption, as the very blessedness of the life of the Son of God, as the only true relation to the Father, and therefore as that which Jesus must give us if we are to have any part with Him, that the terrible lack of actual, heavenly, manifest humility will become a burden and a sorrow, and our ordinary religion be set aside to secure this, the first and the chief of the marks of the Christ within us.

Brother, are you clothed with humility? Ask your daily life. Ask Jesus. Ask your

friends.   Ask the world.   And begin to
praise God that there is opened up to
you in Jesus a heavenly humility of which
you have hardly known, and through
which a heavenly blessedness you possibly have never yet tasted can come in to
you.

IV.

HUMILITY IN THE TEACHING OF JESUS.

"Learn of Me, for I am meek and lowly of heart."—Matt. xi. 29. "Whosoever will be chief among you, let him be your servant, even as the Son of Man came to serve."—Matt. xx. 27.

WE have seen humility in the life of Christ, as He laid open His heart to us: let us listen to His teaching. There we shall hear how He speaks of it, and how far He expects men, and specially His disciples, to be humble as He was. Let us carefully study the passages, which I can scarce do more than quote, to receive the full impression of how often and how earnestly He taught it: it may help us to realize what He asks of us.

1. Look at the commencement of His ministry. In the Beatitudes with which the Sermon on the Mount opens, He speaks : *"Blessed are the poor in spirit; for theirs is the kingdom of heaven. Blessed are the meek; for they shall inherit the earth."* The very first words of His proclamation of the kingdom of heaven reveal the open gate through which alone we enter. The poor, who have nothing in themselves, to them the kingdom comes. The meek, who seek nothing in themselves, theirs the earth shall be. The blessings of heaven and earth are for the lowly. For the heavenly and the earthly life, humility is the secret of blessing.

2. *"Learn of Me; for I am meek and lowly of heart, and ye shall find rest for your souls."* Jesus offers Himself as Teacher. He tells us what the spirit both is, which we shall find in Him as Teacher, and which we can learn and

receive from Him. Meekness and lowliness is the one thing He offers us; in it we shall find perfect rest of soul. Humility is to be our salvation.

3. The disciples had been disputing who would be the greatest in the kingdom, and had agreed to ask the Master (Luke ix. 46; Matt. xviii. 3). He set a child in their midst, and said, "*Whosoever shall humble himself as this little child, shall be exalted.*" "Who is the greatest in the kingdom of heaven?" The question is indeed a far-reaching one. What will be the chief distinction in the heavenly kingdom? The answer, none but Jesus would have given. The chief glory of heaven, the true heavenly-mindedness, the chief of the graces, is humility. "*He that is least among you, the same shall be great.*"

4. The sons of Zebedee had asked Jesus to sit on His right and left, the

highest place in the kingdom. Jesus said it was not His to give, but the Father's, who would give it to those for whom it was prepared. They must not look or ask for it. Their thought must be of the cup and the baptism of humiliation. And then He added, "*Whosoever will be chief among you, let him be your servant. Even as the Son of Man came to serve.*" Humility, as it is the mark of Christ the heavenly, will be the one standard of glory in heaven: the lowliest is the nearest to God. The primacy in the Church is promised to the humblest.

5. Speaking to the multitude and the disciples, of the Pharisees and their love of the chief seats, Christ said once again (Matt. xxiii. 11), "*He that is greatest among you shall be your servant.*" Humiliation is the only ladder to honor in God's kingdom.

6. On another occasion, in the house

of a Pharisee, He spoke the parable of the guest who would be invited to come up higher (Luke xiv. 1–11), and added, *"For whosoever exalteth himself shall be abased; and he that humbleth himself shall be exalted."* The demand is inexorable; there is no other way. Self-abasement alone will be exalted.

7. After the parable of the Pharisee and the Publican, Christ spake again (Luke xviii. 14), *"Every one that exalteth himself shall be abased; and he that humbleth himself shall be exalted."* In the temple and presence and worship of God, everything is worthless that is not pervaded by deep, true humility towards God and men.

8. After washing the disciples' feet, Jesus said (John xiii. 14), *"If I, then, the Lord and Master, have washed your feet, ye also ought to wash one another's feet."* The authority of command and example,

every thought, either of obedience or conformity, make humility the first and most
essential element of discipleship.

9. At the Holy Supper table the disciples still disputed who should be greatest
(Luke xxii. 26).   Jesus said, "*He that is
greatest among you, let him be as the
younger; and he that is chief, as he that
doth serve. I am among you as he that
serveth.*"   The path in which Jesus
walked, and which He opened up for
us, the power and spirit in which He
wrought out salvation, and to which He
saves us, is ever the humility that makes
me the servant of all.

How little this is preached. How little it is practised. How little the lack of
it is felt or confessed. I do not say, how
few attain to it, some recognizable measure of likeness to Jesus in His humility.
But how few ever think of making it a
distinct object of continual desire or

prayer. How little the world has seen
it. How little has it been seen, even in
the inner circle of the Church.

"Whosoever will be chief among you,
let him be your servant." Would God
that it might be given us to believe that
Jesus means this! We all know what the
character of a faithful servant or slave
implies. Devotion to the master's inter-
ests, thoughtful study and care to please
him, delight in his prosperity and honor
and happiness. There are servants on
earth in whom these dispositions have
been seen, and to whom the name of servant has never been anything but a glory.
To how many of us has it not been a new
joy in the Christian life to know that we
may yield ourselves as servants, as slaves
to God, and to find that His service is
our highest liberty,—the liberty from sin
and self ? We need now to learn another
lesson,—that Jesus calls us to be servants

of one another, and that, as we accept
it heartily, this service, too, will be a
most blessed one, a new and fuller liberty, too, from sin and self. At first it
may appear hard: this is only because of
the pride which still counts itself something. If once we learn that to be nothing before God is the glory of the creature, the spirit of Jesus, the joy of heaven,
we shall welcome with our whole heart
the discipline we may have in serving
even those who try or vex us. When
our own heart is set upon this, the true
sanctification, we shall study each word
of Jesus on self-abasement with new zest,
and no place will be too low, and no
stooping too deep, and no service too
mean or too long-continued, if we may
but share and prove the fellowship with
Him who spake, "I am among you as he
that serveth."

Brethren, here is the path to the

higher life. Down, lower down! This was what Jesus ever said to the disciples who were thinking of being great in the kingdom, and of sitting on His right hand and His left. Seek not, ask not for exaltation; that is God's work. Look to it that you abase and humble yourselves, and take no place before God or man but that of servant; that is your work; let that be your one purpose and prayer. God is faithful. Just as water ever seeks and fills the lowest place, so the moment God finds the creature abased and empty, His glory and power flow in to exalt and to bless. He that humbleth himself—that must be our one care —shall be exalted; that is God's care; by His mighty power and in His great love He will do it.

Men sometimes speak as if humility and meekness would rob us of what is noble and bold and manlike. Oh, that all would believe that this is the nobility of the kingdom of heaven, that this is the royal spirit that the King of heaven displayed, that this is Godlike, to humble oneself, to become the servant of all! This is the path to the gladness and the glory of Christ's presence ever in us, His power ever resting on us.

Jesus, the meek and lowly One, calls us to learn of Him the path to God. Let us study the words we have been reading, until our heart is filled with the thought: My one need is humility. And let us believe that what He shows, He gives, what He is, He imparts. As the meek and lowly One, He will come in and dwell in the longing heart.

V.

HUMILITY IN THE DISCIPLES OF JESUS.

"Let him that is chief among you be as he that doth serve."—LUKE xxii. 26.

WE have studied humility in the person and teaching of Jesus; let us now look for it in the circle of His chosen companions—the twelve apostles. If, in the lack of it, we find in them the contrast between Christ and men is brought out more clearly, it will help us to appreciate the mighty change which Pentecost wrought in them, and prove how real our participation can be in the perfect triumph of Christ's humility over the pride Satan had breathed into man.

In the texts quoted from the teaching of Jesus, we have already seen what the occasions were on which the disciples had proved how entirely wanting they were in the grace of humility. Once they had been disputing by the way which of them should be the greatest. Another time the sons of Zebedee with their mother had asked for the first places—the seat on the right hand and the left. And, later on, at the Supper table on the last night, there was again a contention which should be accounted the greatest. Not that there were not moments when they indeed humbled themselves before their Lord. So it was with Peter when he cried out, "Depart from me, O Lord, for I am a sinful man." So, too, with the disciples when they fell down and worshipped Him who had stilled the storm. But such occasional expressions of humility only bring out into stronger relief what was the habitual tone of their mind, as shown in the natural and spontaneous revelation given at other times of the place and the power of self. The study of the meaning of all this will teach us most important lessons.

First, *How much there may be of earnest and active religion while humility is still sadly wanting.*—See it in the disciples. There was in them fervent attachment to Jesus. They had forsaken all for Him. The Father had revealed to them that He was the Christ of God. They believed in Him, they loved Him, they obeyed His commandments. They had forsaken all to follow Him. When others went back, they clave to Him. They were ready to die with Him. But deeper down than all this there was a dark power, of the existence and the hideousness of which they were hardly conscious, which had to be slain and

cast out, ere they could be the witnesses
of the power of Jesus to save. It is even
so still. We may find professors and
ministers, evangelists and workers, mis-
sionaries and teachers, in whom the gifts
of the Spirit are many and manifest, and
who are the channels of blessing to multitudes, but of whom, when the testing
time comes, or closer intercourse gives
fuller knowledge, it is only too painfully
manifest that the grace of humility, as an
abiding characteristic, is scarce to be
seen. All tends to confirm the lesson
that humility is one of the chief and the
highest graces; one of the most difficult
of attainment; one to which our first and
chiefest efforts ought to be directed; one
that only comes in power, when the fullness of the Spirit makes us partakers of
the indwelling Christ, and He lives
within us.

Second, *How impotent all external*

*teaching and all personal effort is, to con-
quer pride or give the meek and lowly
heart.*—For three years the disciples had
been in the training school of Jesus. He
had told them what the chief lesson was
He wished to teach them : "Learn of
Me, for I am meek and lowly in heart."
Time after time He had spoken to them,
to the Pharisees, to the multitude, of humility as the only path to the glory of
God. He had not only lived before
them as the Lamb of God in His divine
humility, He had more than once un-
folded to them the inmost secret of His
life: "The Son of Man came not to be
served, but so serve"; "I am among you
as one that serveth." He had washed
their feet, and told them they were to
follow His example. And yet all had
availed but little. At the Holy Supper
there was still the contention as to who
should be greatest. They had doubtless

often tried to learn His lessons, and firmly resolved not again to grieve Him. But all in vain. To teach them and us the much-needed lesson, that no outward instruction, not even of Christ Himself; no argument, however convincing ; no sense of the beauty of humility, however deep; no personal resolve or effort, however sincere and earnest,—can cast out the devil of pride. When Satan casts out Satan, it is only to enter afresh in a mightier, though more hidden power. Nothing can avail but this, that the new nature in its divine humility be revealed in power to take the place of the old, to become as truly our very nature as that ever was.

Third, *It is only by the indwelling of Christ in His divine humility that we become truly humble.*—We have our pride from another, from Adam; we must have our humility from Another too.   Pride is ours, and rules in us with such terrible power, because it is ourself, our very nature. Humility must be ours in the same way; it must be our very self, our very nature. As natural and easy as it has been to be proud, it must be, it will be, to be humble. The promise is, "Where," even in the heart, "sin abounded, grace did abound more exceedingly." All Christ's teaching of His disciples, and all their vain efforts, were the needful preparation for His entering into them in divine power, to give and be in them what He had taught them to desire. In His death He destroyed the power of the devil, He put away sin, and effected an everlasting redemption. In His resurrection He received from the Father an entirely new life, the life of man in the power of God, capable of being communicated to men, and entering and renewing and filling their lives with His divine

power. In His ascension He received
the Spirit of the Father, through whom
He might do what He could not do while
upon earth, make Himself one with those
He loved, actually live their life for them,
so that they could live before the Father
in a humility like His, because it was
Himself who lived and breathed in them.
And on Pentecost He came and took
possession. The work of preparation and
conviction, the awakening of desire and
hope which His teaching had effected,
was perfected by the mighty change that
Pentecost wrought. And the lives and
the epistles of James and Peter and John
bear witness that all was changed, and
that the spirit of the meek and suffering
Jesus had indeed possession of them.

What shall we say to these things?
Among my readers I am sure there is
more than one class. There may be some
who have never yet thought very specially

of the matter, and cannot at once realize
its immense importance as a life question
for the Church and its every member.
There are others who have felt condemned for their shortcomings, and have
put forth very earnest efforts, only to fail
and be discouraged. Others, again, may
be able to give joyful testimony of spiritual blessing and power, and yet there has
never been the needed conviction of what
those around them still see as wanting.
And still others may be able to witness
that in regard to this grace too the Lord
has given deliverance and victory, while
He has taught them how much they still
need and may expect out of the fullness
of Jesus. To whichever class we belong,
may I urge the pressing need there is for
our all seeking a still deeper conviction
of the unique place that humility holds
in the religion of Christ, and the utter
impossibility of the Church or the be-

liever being what Christ would have them be, as long as *His humility is not recognized as His chief glory, His first command, and our highest blessedness.* Let us consider deeply how far the disciples were advanced while this grace was still so terribly lacking, and let us pray to God that other gifts may not so satisfy us, that we never grasp the fact that the absence of this grace is the secret cause why the power of God cannot do its mighty work. It is only where we, like the Son, truly know and show that we can do nothing of ourselves, that God will do all.

It is when the truth of an indwelling Christ takes the place it claims in the experience of believers, that the Church will put on her beautiful garments, and humility be seen in her teachers and members as the beauty of holiness.

VI.

HUMILITY IN DAILY LIFE.

"He that loveth not his brother whom he hath seen, how can he love God whom he hath not seen?"—1 John iv. 20.

WHAT a solemn thought, that our love to God will be measured by our everyday intercourse with men and the love it displays; and that our love to God will be found to be a delusion, except as its truth is proved in standing the test of daily life with our fellow-men. It is even so with our humility. It is easy to think we humble ourselves before God: humility towards men will be the only sufficient proof that our humility before God is real; that humility has taken up its abode

in us, and become our very nature; that
we actually, like Christ, have made ourselves of no reputation. When in the
presence of God lowliness of heart has
become, not a posture we assume for a
time, when we think of Him, or pray to
Him, but the very spirit of our life, it will
manifest itself in all our bearing towards
our brethren.   The lesson is one of deep
import: the only humility that is really
ours is not that which we try to show before God in prayer, but that which we
carry with us, and carry out, in our ordinary conduct; the insignificances of daily
life are the importances and the tests of
eternity, because they prove what really
is the spirit that possesses us. It is in
our most unguarded moments that we
really show and see what we are. To
know the humble man, to know how the
humble man behaves, you must follow
him in the common course of daily life.

Is not this what Jesus taught? It was when the disciples disputed who should be greatest; when He saw how the Pharisees loved the chief place at feasts and the chief seats in the synagogues; when He had given them the example of washing their feet,—that He taught His lessons of humility. Humility before God is nothing if not proved in humility before men.

It is even so in the teaching of Paul. To the Romans He writes: "In honor preferring *one another*"; "Set not your mind on high things, but condescend to *those that are lowly*"; "Be not wise in your own conceit." To the Corinthians: "Love," and there is no love without humility as its root, "vaunteth not itself, is not puffed up, seeketh not its own, is not provoked." To the Galatians: "Through love be servants *one of another*. Let us not be desirous of vainglory, pro-

voking *one another*, envying *one another*."
To the Ephesians, immediately after the
three wonderful chapters on the heavenly
life: "Therefore, walk with all lowliness
and meekness, with long-suffering, forbearing *one another* in love"; "Giving
thanks always, subjecting yourselves *one
to another* in the fear of Christ." To the
Philippians : "Doing nothing through
faction or vainglory, but in lowliness o
mind, each counting *other* better than
himself. Have the mind in you which
was also in Christ Jesus, who emptied
Himself, taking the form of a servant,
and humbled Himself." And to the
Colossians : "Put on a heart of compassion, kindness, humility, meekness, long-
suffering, forbearing *one another*, and
forgiving *each other*, even as the Lord
forgave you." It is in our relation to one
another, in our treatment of one another,
that the true lowliness of mind and **the**

heart of humility are to be seen. Our humility before God has no value, but as it prepares us to reveal the humility of Jesus to our fellow-men. Let us study humility in daily life in the light of these words.

The humble man seeks at all times to act up to the rule, "*In honor preferring one another; Servants one of another; Each counting others better than himself; Subjecting yourselves one to another.*" The question is often asked, how we can count others better than ourselves, when we see that they are far below us in wisdom and in holiness, in natural gifts, or in grace received. The question proves at once how little we understand what real lowliness of mind is. True humility comes when, in the light of God, we have seen ourselves to be nothing, have consented to part with and cast away self, to let God be all. The soul that has done this, and can say, So have I lost myself in finding Thee, no longer compares itself with others. It has given up forever every thought of self in God's presence; it meets its fellow-men as one who is nothing, and seeks nothing for itself; who is a servant of God, and for His sake a servant of all. A faithful servant may be wiser than the master, and yet retain the true spirit and posture of the servant. The humble man looks upon every, the feeblest and unworthiest, child of God, and honors him and prefers him in honor as the son of a King. The spirit of Him who washed the disciples' feet, makes it a joy to us to be indeed the least, to be servants one of another.

The humble man feels no jealousy or envy. He can praise God when others are preferred and blessed before him. He can bear to hear others praised and himself forgotten, because in God's presence he has learned to say with Paul, " I am nothing." He has received the spirit of Jesus, who pleased not Himself, and sought not His own honor, as the spirit of his life.

Amid what are considered the temptations to impatience and touchiness, to hard thoughts and sharp words, which come from the failings and sins of fellow-Christians, the humble man carries the oft-repeated injunction in his heart, and shows it in his life, " *Forbearing one another, and forgiving one another, even as the Lord forgave you.*" He has learned that in putting on the Lord Jesus he *has put on the heart of compassion, kindness, humility, meekness, and long-suffering.* Jesus has taken the place of self, and it is not an impossibility to forgive as Jesus forgave. His humility does not consist merely in thoughts or words of self-depreciation, but, as Paul puts it, in " a heart of humility," encompassed by compassion and kindness, meekness and long-suffering,—the sweet and lowly gentleness recognized as the mark of the Lamb of God.

In striving after the higher experiences of the Christian life, the believer is often in danger of aiming at and rejoicing in what one might call the more human, the manly, virtues, such as boldness, joy, contempt of the world, zeal, self-sacrifice,—even the old Stoics taught and practised these,—while the deeper and gentler, the diviner and more heavenly graces, those which Jesus first taught upon earth, because He brought them from heaven; those which are more distinctly connected with His cross and the death of self,—poverty of spirit, meekness, humility, lowliness,—are scarcely thought of or valued. Therefore, let us put on a heart of compassion, kindness, humility, meekness, long-suffering; and let us prove our Christ-likeness, not only in our zeal for saving the lost, but before all in our intercourse with the brethren, forbearing and forgiving one another, *even as the Lord forgave us.*

Fellow-Christians, do let us study the Bible portrait of the humble man. And let us ask our brethren, and ask the world, whether they recognize in us the likeness to the original. Let us be content with nothing less than taking each of these texts as the promise of what God will work in us, as the revelation in words of what the Spirit of Jesus will give as a birth within us. And let each failure and shortcoming simply urge us to turn humbly and meekly to the meek and lowly lamb of God, in the assurance that where He is enthroned in the heart, His humility and gentleness will be one of the streams of living water that flow from within us.[1]

Once again I repeat what I have said before. I feel deeply that we have very little conception of what the Church suffers from the lack of this divine humility, —the nothingness that makes room for God to prove His power. It is not long since a Christian, of an humble, loving spirit, acquainted with not a few mission stations of various societies, expressed his deep sorrow that in some cases the spirit of love and forbearance was sadly

---

[1] "I knew Jesus, and He was very precious to my soul: but I found something in me that would not keep sweet and patient and kind. I did what I could to keep it down, but it was there. I besought Jesus to do something for me, and when I gave Him my will, He came to my heart, and took out all that would not be sweet, all that would not be kind, all that would not be patient, and then He shut the door."— GEORGE FOXE.

lacking. Men and women, who in Europe could each choose their own circle of friends, brought close together with others of uncongenial minds, find it hard to bear, and to love, and to keep the unity of the Spirit in the bond of peace. And those who should have been fellow-helpers of each other's joy, became a hindrance and a weariness. And all for the one reason, the lack of the humility which counts itself nothing, which rejoices in becoming and being counted the least, and only seeks, like Jesus, to be the servant, the helper and comforter of others, even the lowest and unworthiest.

And whence comes it that men who have joyfully given up themselves for Christ, find it so hard to give up themselves for their brethren? Is not the blame with the Church? It has so little taught its sons that the humility of Christ is the first of the virtues, the best of all

the graces and powers of the Spirit. It
has so little proved that a Christlike
humility is what it, like Christ, places
and preaches first, as what is in very deed
needed, and possible too. But let us not
be discouraged. Let the discovery of
the lack of this grace stir us to larger
expectation from God. Let us look upon
every brother who tries or vexes us, as
God's means of grace, God's instrument
for our purification, for our exercise of
the humility Jesus our Life breathes
within us. And let us have such faith in
the All of God, and the nothing of self,
that, as nothing in our own eyes, we may,
in God's power, only seek to serve one
another in love.

VII.

HUMILITY AND HOLINESS.

"Which say, Stand by thyself; for I am holier than thou."—ISAIAH lxv. 5.

WE speak of the Holiness movement in our times, and praise God for it. We hear a great deal of seekers after holiness and professors of holiness, of holiness teaching and holiness meetings. The blessed truths of holiness in Christ, and holiness by faith, are being emphasized as never before. The great test of whether the holiness we profess to seek or to attain, is truth and life, will be *whether it be manifest in the increasing humility it produces.* In the creature, humility is

(73)

the one thing needed to allow God's holiness to dwell in him and shine through him. In Jesus, the Holy One of God who makes us holy, a divine humility was the secret of His life and His death and His exaltation; the one infallible test of our holiness will be the humility before God and men which marks us. Humility is the bloom and the beauty of holiness.

The chief mark of counterfeit holiness is its lack of humility. Every seeker after holiness needs to be on his guard, lest unconsciously what was begun in the spirit be perfected in the flesh, and pride creep in where its presence is least expected. Two men went up into the temple to pray: the one a Pharisee, the other a publican. There is no place or position so sacred but the Pharisee can enter there. Pride can lift its head in the very temple of God, and make His worship the scene of its self-exaltation. Since the time

Christ so exposed his pride, the Pharisee has put on the garb of the publican, and the confessor of deep sinfulness equally with the professor of the highest holiness, must be on the watch. Just when we are most anxious to have our heart the temple of God, we shall find the two men coming up to pray. And the publican will find that his danger is not from the Pharisee beside him, who despises him, but the Pharisee within who commends and exalts. In God's temple, when we think we are in the holiest of all, in the presence of His holiness, let us beware of pride. "Now there was a day when the sons of God came to present themselves before the Lord, and Satan came also among them."

"God, I thank Thee, I am not as the rest of men, or even as this publican." It is in that which is just cause for thanksgiving, it is in the very thanksgiv-

ing which we render to God, it may be
in the very confession that God has done
it all, that self finds its cause of complacency. Yes, even when in the temple
the language of penitence and trust in
God's mercy alone is heard, the Pharisee
may take up the note of praise, and in
thanking God be congratulating himself.
Pride can clothe itself in the garments of
praise or of penitence. Even though the
words, "I am not as the rest of men," are
rejected and condemned, their spirit may
too often be found in our feelings and
language towards our fellow-worshippers
and fellow-men. Would you know if this
really is so, just listen to the way in which
Churches and Christians often speak of
one another. How little of the meekness
and gentleness of Jesus is to be seen. It
is so little remembered that deep humility must be the keynote of what the
servants of Jesus say of themselves or

each other. Is there not many a Church
or assembly of the saints, many a mission
or convention, many a society or com-
mittee, even many a mission away in
heathendom, where the harmony has been
disturbed and the work of God hindered,
because men who are counted saints have
proved in touchiness and haste and impatience, in self-defense and self-assertion, in sharp judgments and unkind
words, that they did not each reckon
others better than themselves, and that
their holiness has but little in it of the
meekness of the saints?[1] In their spirit-

---

[1] "ME is a most exacting personage, requir-
ing the best seat and the highest place for itself,
and feeling grievously wounded if its claim is
not recognized. Most of the quarrels among
Christian workers arise from the clamoring of
this gigantic ME. How few of us understand
the true secret of taking our seats in the lowest
rooms."—MRS. SMITH, *Everyday Religion.*

ual history men may have had times of
great humbling and brokenness, but what
a different thing this is from being clothed
with humility, from having an humble
spirit, from having that lowliness of mind
in which each counts himself the servant
of others, and so shows forth the very
mind which was also in Jesus Christ.

"*Stand by; for I am holier than thou!*"
What a parody on holiness! Jesus the
Holy One is the humble one : the holiest
will ever be the humblest. There is none
holy but God : we have as much of holiness as we have of God. And accord-
ing to what we have of God will be our
real humility, because humility is nothing
but the disappearance of self in the vision
that God is all. The holiest will be the
humblest. Alas! though the barefaced
boasting Jew of the days of Isaiah is not
often to be found,—even our manners
have taught us not to speak thus,—how

often his spirit is still seen, whether in the treatment of fellow-saints or of the children of the world. In the spirit in which opinions are given, and work is undertaken, and faults are exposed, how often, though the garb be that of the publican, the voice is still that of the Pharisee: "O God, I thank Thee that I am not as other men."

And is there, then, such humility to be found, that men shall indeed still count themselves "less than the least of all saints," the servants of all? There is. "Love vaunteth not itself, is not puffed up, seeketh not its own." Where the spirit of love is shed abroad in the heart, where the divine nature comes to a full birth, where Christ the meek and lowly Lamb of God is truly formed within, there is given the power of a perfect love that forgets itself and finds its blessedness in blessing others, in bearing with them and honoring them, however feeble they be. Where this love enters, there God enters. And where God has entered in His power, and reveals Himself as All, there the creature becomes nothing. And where the creature becomes nothing before God, it cannot be anything but humble towards the fellow-creature. The presence of God becomes not a thing of times and seasons, but the covering under which the soul ever dwells, and its deep abasement before God becomes the holy place of His presence whence all its words and works proceed.

May God teach us that our thoughts and words and feelings concerning our fellow-men are His test of our humility towards Him, and that our humility before Him is the only power that can enable us to be always humble with our fellow-men. Our humility must be the life of Christ, the Lamb of God, within us.

Let all teachers of holiness, whether in the pulpit or on the platform, and all seekers after holiness, whether in the closet or the convention, take warning. There is no pride so dangerous, because none so subtle and insidious, as the pride of holiness. It is not that a man ever says, or even thinks, "Stand by; I am holier than thou." No, indeed, the thought would be regarded with abhorrence. But there grows up, all unconsciously, a hidden habit of soul, which feels complacency in its attainments, and cannot help seeing how far it is in advance of others. It can be recognized, not always in any special self-assertion or self-laudation, but simply in the absence of that deep self-abasement which cannot but be the mark of the soul that has seen the glory of God (Job xlii. 5, 6 ; Isa. vi. 5). It reveals itself, not only in words or thoughts, but in a tone, a way of

speaking of others, in which those who
have the gift of spiritual discernment
cannot but recognize the power of self.
Even the world with its keen eyes notices
it, and points to it as a proof that the
profession of a heavenly life does not
bear any specially heavenly fruits. O
brethren! let us beware. Unless we
make, with each advance in what we
think holiness, the increase of humility
our study, we may find that we have been
delighting in beautiful thoughts and feelings, in solemn acts of consecration and
faith, while the only sure mark of the
presence of God, the disappearance of
self, was all the time wanting. Come and
let us flee to Jesus, and hide ourselves in
Him until we be clothed upon with His
humility.   That alone is our holiness.

VIII.

HUMILITY AND SIN.

"Sinners, of whom I am chief."—1 TIM. i. 15.

HUMILITY is often identified with penitence and contrition. As a consequence,
there appears to be no way of fostering
humility but by keeping the soul occupied with its sin. We have learned, I
think, that humility is something else
and something more. We have seen in
the teaching of our Lord Jesus and the
Epistles how often the virtue is incul-
cated without any reference to sin. In
the very nature of things, in the whole
relation of the creature to the Creator, in
the life of Jesus as He lived it and imparts it to us, humility is the very essence
of holiness as of blessedness. It is the

displacement of self by the enthronement of God. Where God is all, self is nothing.

But though it is this aspect of the truth I have felt it specially needful to press, I need scarce say what new depth and intensity man's sin and God's grace give to the humility of the saints. We have only to look at a man like the Apostle Paul, to see how, through his life as a ransomed and a holy man, the deep consciousness of having been a sinner lives inextinguishably. We all know the passages in which he refers to his life as a persecutor and blasphemer. "I am *the least of the apostles*, that am *not worthy to be called an apostle*, because I persecuted the Church of God. . . . . I labored more abundantly than they all; yet not I, but the grace of God which was with me" (1 Cor. xv. 9, 10). "Unto me, who am *less than the least of all saints*, was this grace given, to preach to the heathen" (Eph. iii. 8). "I was before *a blasphemer, and a persecutor, and injurious;* howbeit I obtained mercy, because I did it ignorantly in unbelief. . . . . Christ Jesus came unto the world to save *sinners, of whom I am chief*" (1 Tim. i. 13, 15). God's grace had saved him; God remembered his sins no more forever; but never, never could he forget how terribly he had sinned. The more he rejoiced in God's salvation, and the more his experience of God's grace filled him with joy unspeakable, the clearer was his consciousness that he was a saved sinner, and that salvation had no meaning or sweetness except as the sense of his being a sinner made it precious and real to him. Never for a moment could he forget that it was a sinner God had taken up in His arms and crowned with His love.

The texts we have just quoted are often

appealed to as Paul's confession of daily
sinning. One has only to read them carefully in their connection, to see how little
this is the case. They have a far deeper
meaning, they refer to that which lasts
throughout eternity, and which will give
its deep undertone of amazement and
adoration to the humility with which the
ransomed bow before the throne, as those
who have been washed from their sins in
the blood of the Lamb. Never, never,
even in glory, can they be other than
ransomed sinners ; never for a moment
in this life can God's child live in the full
light of His love, but as he feels that the
sin, out of which he has been saved, is
his one only right and title to all that
grace has promised to do. The humility
with which first he came as a sinner, ac-
quires a new meaning when he learns
how it becomes him as a creature. And
then ever again, the humility, in which

he was born as a creature, has its deepest, richest tones of adoration, in the memory of what it is to be a monument of God's wondrous redeeming love.

The true import of what these expressions of St. Paul teach us comes out all the more strongly when we notice the remarkable fact that, through his whole Christian course, we never find from his pen, even in those epistles in which we have the most intensely personal unbosomings, anything like confession of sin. Nowhere is there any mention of shortcoming or defect, nowhere any suggestion to his readers that he has failed in duty, or sinned against the law of perfect love. On the contrary, there are passages not a few in which he vindicates himself in language that means nothing if it does not appeal to a faultless life before God and men. "Ye are witnesses, and God also, how holily, and righteously, and un-

blameably we behaved ourselves toward
you" (1 Thess. ii. 10). "Our glorying
is this, the testimony of our conscience,
that in holiness and sincerity of God we
behaved ourselves in the world, and more
abundantly to you-ward" (2 Cor. i. 12).
This is not an ideal or an inspiration ; it
is an appeal to what his actual life had
been.   However we may account for this
absence of confession of sin, all will ad-
mit that it must point to a life in the
power of the Holy Ghost, such as is but
seldom realized or expected in these our
days.

The point which I wish to emphasize
is this—that the very fact of the absence
of such confession of sinning only gives
the more force to the truth that it is not
in daily sinning that the secret of the
deeper humility will be found, but in the
habitual, never for a moment to be forgotten position, which just the more

abundant grace will keep more distinctly alive, that our only place, the only place of blessing, our one abiding position before God, must be that of those whose highest joy it is to confess that they are sinners saved by grace.

With Paul's deep remembrance of having sinned so terribly in the past, ere grace had met him, and the consciousness of being kept from present sinning, there was ever coupled the abiding remembrance of the dark hidden power of sin ever ready to come in, and only kept out by the presence and power of the indwelling Christ. "In me, that is, in my flesh, dwelleth no good thing";—these words of Rom. vii. describe the flesh as it is to the end. The glorious deliverance of Rom. viii.—"The law of the Spirit of life in Christ Jesus hath now made me free from the law of sin, which once led me captive "—is neither the an-

nihilation nor the sanctification of the
flesh, but a continuous victory given by
the Spirit as He mortifies the deeds of
the body.   As health expels disease, and
light swallows up darkness, and life con-
quers death, the indwelling of Christ
through the Spirit is the health and light
and life of the soul.   But with this, the
conviction of helplessness and danger
ever tempers the faith in the momentary
and unbroken action of the Holy Spirit
into that chastened sense of dependence
which makes the highest faith and joy
the handmaids of a humility that only
lives by the grace of God.

The three passages above quoted all
show that it was the wonderful grace bestowed upon Paul, and of which he felt
the need every moment, that humbled
him so deeply.   The grace of God that
was with him, and enabled him to labor
more abundantly than they all ; the grace

to preach to the heathen the unsearchable riches of Christ ; the grace that was exceeding abundant with faith and love which is in Christ Jesus,—it was this grace of which it is the very nature and glory that it is for sinners, that kept the consciousness of his having once sinned, and being liable to sin, so intensely alive. "Where sin abounded, grace did abound more exceedingly." This reveals how the very essence of grace is to deal with and take away sin, and how it must ever be : the more abundant the experience of grace, the more intense the consciousness of being a sinner. It is not sin, but God's grace showing a man and ever reminding him what a sinner he was, that will keep him truly humble. It is not sin, but grace, that will make me indeed know myself a sinner, and make the sinner's place of deepest self-abasement the place I never leave.

I fear that there are not a few who, by strong expressions of self-condemnation and self-denunciation, have sought to humble themselves, and have to confess with sorrow that a humble spirit, a " heart of humility," with its accompaniments of kindness and compassion, of meekness and forbearance, is still as far off as ever. Being occupied with self, even amid the deepest self-abhorrence, can never free us from self. It is the revelation of God, not only by the law condemning sin, but by His grace delivering from it, that will make us humble. The law may break the heart with fear , it is only grace that works that sweet humility which becomes a joy to the soul as its second nature. It was the revelation of God in His holiness, drawing nigh to make Himself known in His grace, that made Abraham and Jacob, Job and Isaiah, bow so low. It is the soul in which God the Creator,

as the All of the creature in its nothingness, God the Redeemer in His grace, as
the All of the sinner in his sinfulness, is
waited for and trusted and worshipped,
that will find itself so filled with His
presence, that there will be no place for
self. So alone can the promise be fulfilled : "The haughtiness of man shall
be brought low, and the Lord alone be
exalted in that day."

It is the sinner dwelling in the full
light of God's holy, redeeming love, in
the experience of that full indwelling of
divine love, which comes through Christ
and the Holy Spirit, who cannot but be
humble. Not to be occupied with thy
sin, but to be occupied with God, brings
deliverance from self.

IX.

HUMILITY AND FAITH.

"How can ye believe, which receive glory
from one another, and the glory that cometh
from the only God ye seek not?"—John iv. 44.

In an address I lately heard, the speaker
said that the blessings of the higher
Christian life were often like the objects
exposed in a shop window,—one could
see them clearly, and yet could not reach
them. If told to stretch out his hand
and take, a man would answer, I cannot;
there is a thick pane of plate-glass between me and them. And even so Christians may see clearly the blessed promises
of perfect peace and rest, of overflowing

love and joy, of abiding communion and
fruitfulness, and yet feel that there was
something between, hindering the true
possession. And what might that be?
Nothing but pride. The promises made
to faith are so free and sure; the invita-
tions and encouragements so strong; the
mighty power of God on which it may
count is so near and free,—that it can
only be something that hinders faith that
hinders the blessing being ours. In our
text Jesus discovers to us that it is indeed
pride that makes faith impossible. "How
can ye believe, which receive glory from
one another?" As we see how in their
very nature pride and faith are irrecon-
cilably at variance, we shall learn that
faith and humility are at root one, and
that we never can have more of true faith
than we have of true humility; we shall
see that we may indeed have strong in-
tellectual conviction and assurance of the

truth while pride is kept in the heart, but that it makes the living faith, which has power with God, an impossibility.

We need only think for a moment what faith is. Is it not the confession of nothingness and helplessness, the surrender and the waiting to let God work? Is it not in itself the most humbling thing there can be,—the acceptance of our place as dependents, who can claim or get or do nothing but what grace bestows? Humility is simply the disposition which prepares the soul for living on trust. And every, even the most secret breathing of pride, in self-seeking, self-will, self-confidence, or self-exaltation, is just the strengthening of that self which cannot enter the kingdom, or possess the things of the kingdom, because it refuses to allow God to be what He is and must be there—the All in All.

Faith is the organ or sense for the per-

ception and apprehension of the heavenly
world and its blessings. Faith seeks the
glory that comes from God, that only
comes where God is All. As long as we
take glory from one another, as long as
ever we seek and love and jealously
guard the glory of this life, the honor
and reputation that comes from men, we
do not seek, and cannot receive the glory
that comes from God. Pride renders
faith impossible. Salvation comes through
a cross and a crucified Christ. Salvation
is the fellowship with the crucified Christ
in the spirit of His cross. Salvation is
union with and delight in, salvation is
participation in, the humility of Jesus.
Is it wonder that our faith is so feeble
when pride still reigns so much, and we
have scarce learned even to long or pray
for humility as the most needful and
blessed part of salvation?

Humility and faith are more nearly

allied in Scripture than many know. See
it in the life of Christ. There are two
cases in which He spoke of a great faith.
Had not the centurion, at whose faith
He marvelled, saying, "I have not found
so great faith, no, not in Israel!" spoken,
"*I am not worthy* that Thou shouldst
come under my roof"? And had not the
mother to whom He spoke, "O woman,
great is thy faith!" accepted the name of
dog, and said, "*Yea, Lord, yet the dogs eat
of the crumbs*"? It is the humility that
brings a soul to be nothing before God,
that also removes every hindrance to
faith, and makes it only fear lest it
should dishonor Him by not trusting Him
wholly.

Brother, have we not here the cause of
failure in the pursuit of holiness? Is it
not this, though we knew it not, that
made our consecration and our faith so
superficial and so short-lived? We had

no idea to what an extent pride and self were still secretly working within us, and how alone God by His incoming and His mighty power could cast them out. We understood not how nothing but the new and divine nature, taking entirely the place of the old self, could make us really humble. We knew not that absolute, unceasing, universal humility must be the root-disposition of every prayer and every approach to God as well as of every dealing with man; and that we might as well attempt to see without eyes, or live without breath, as believe or draw nigh to God or dwell in His love, without an all-pervading humility and lowliness of heart.

Brother, have we not been making a mistake in taking so much trouble to believe, while all the time there was the old self in its pride seeking to possess itself of God's blessing and riches? No won-

der we could not believe. Let us change
our course. Let us seek first of all to
humble ourselves under the mighty hand
of God : *He will exalt us.* The cross,
and the death, and the grave, into which
Jesus humbled Himself, were His path
to the glory of God. And they are our
path. Let our one desire and our fervent
prayer be, to be humbled with Him and
like Him; let us accept gladly whatever
can humble us before God or men;—this
alone is the path to the glory of God.

You perhaps feel inclined to ask a
question. I have spoken of some who
have blessed experiences, or are the means
of bringing blessing to others, and yet
are lacking in humility. You ask whether
these do not prove that they have true,
even strong faith, though they show too
clearly that they still seek too much the
honor that cometh from men. There is
more than one answer can be given. But

the principal answer in our present connection is this : They indeed have a
measure of faith, in proportion to which,
with the special gifts bestowed upon them,
is the blessing they bring to others. But
in that very blessing the work of their
faith is hindered through the lack of
humility. The blessing is often superficial or transitory, just because they are
not the nothing that opens the way for
God to be all. A deeper humility would
without doubt bring a deeper and fuller
blessing. The Holy Spirit not only working in them as a Spirit of power, but
dwelling in them in the fullness of His
grace, and specially that of humility,
would through them communicate Himself to these converts for a life of power
and holiness and steadfastness now all
too little seen.

"How can ye believe, which receive
glory from one another?" Brother!

nothing can cure you of the desire of receiving glory from men, or of the sensitiveness and pain and anger which come when it is not given, but giving yourself to seek only the glory that comes from God. Let the glory of the All-glorious God be everything to you. You will be freed from the glory of men and of self, and be content and glad to be nothing. Out of this nothingness you will grow strong in faith, giving glory to God, and you will find that the deeper you sink in humility before Him, the nearer He is to fulfill the every desire of your faith.

X.

HUMILITY AND DEATH TO SELF.

"He humbled Himself and became obedient unto death."—PHIL. ii. 8.

HUMILITY is the path to death, because in death it gives the highest proof of its perfection. Humility is the blossom of which death to self is the perfect fruit. Jesus humbled Himself unto death, and opened the path in which we too must walk. As there was no way for Him to prove His surrender to God to the very uttermost, or to give up and rise out of fallen human nature to the glory of the Father but through death, so with us too. Humility must lead us to die to self: so

we prove how wholly we have given ourselves up to it and to God; so alone we
are freed from fallen nature, and find the
path that leads to life in God, to that full
birth of the new nature, of which humility is the breath and the joy.

We have spoken of what Jesus did for
His disciples when He communicated
His resurrection life to them, when in the
descent of the Holy Spirit He, the glorified and enthroned Meekness, actually
came from heaven Himself to dwell in
them. He won the power to do this
through death: in its inmost nature the
life He imparted was a life out of death,
a life that had been surrendered to death,
and been won through death. He who
came to dwell in them was Himself One
who had been dead and now lives for
evermore. His life, His person, His
presence, bears the marks of death, of
being a life begotten out of death. That

life in His disciples ever bears the death-marks too; it is only as the Spirit of the death, of the dying One, dwells and works in the soul, that the power of His life can be known. The first and chief of the marks of the dying of the Lord Jesus, of the death-marks that show the true follower of Jesus, is humility. For these two reasons: Only humility leads to perfect death; Only death perfects humility. Humility and death are in their very nature one: humility is the bud; in death the fruit is ripened to perfection.

Humility leads to perfect death.—Humility means the giving up of self, and the taking of the place of perfect nothingness before God. Jesus humbled Himself, and became obedient unto death. In death He gave the highest, the perfect proof of having given up His will to the will of God. In death He gave up His

self, with its natural reluctance to drink
the cup; He gave up the life He had in
union with our fallen nature; He died to
self, and the sin that tempted Him; so,
as man, He entered into the perfect life
of God. If it had not been for His
boundless humility, counting Himself as
nothing except as a servant to do and
suffer the will of God, He never would
have died.

This gives us the answer to the question so often asked, and of which the
meaning is so seldom clearly apprehended:
How can I die to self? The death to
self is not your work, it is God's work.
In Christ *you are dead* to sin; the life
there is in you has gone through the pro-
cess of death and resurrection; you may
be sure you are indeed dead to sin. But
the full manifestation of the power of this
death in your disposition and conduct,
depends upon the measure in which the

Holy Spirit imparts the power of the
death of Christ. And here it is that the
teaching is needed : if you would enter
into full fellowship with Christ in His
death, and know the full deliverance from
self, humble yourself. This is your one
duty. Place yourself before God in your
utter helplessness; consent heartily to the
fact of your impotence to slay or make
alive yourself; sink down into your own
nothingness, in the spirit of meek and
patient and trustful surrender to God.
Accept every humiliation, look upon every
fellow-man who tries or vexes you, as a
means of grace to humble you. Use
every opportunity of humbling yourself
before your fellow-men as a help to abide
humble before God. God will accept
such humbling of yourself as the proof
that your whole heart desires it, as the
very best prayer for it, as your preparation for His mighty work of grace, when,

by the mighty strengthening of His Holy
Spirit, He reveals Christ fully in you, so
that He, in His form of a servant, is truly
formed in you, and dwells in your heart.
It is the path of humility leads to perfect
death, the full and perfect experience
that we are dead in Christ.

Then follows: *Only this death leads to
perfect humility.* Oh, beware of the mistake so many make, who would fain be
humble, but are afraid to be too humble.
They have so many qualifications and
limitations, so many reasonings and ques-
tionings, as to what true humility is to be
and to do, that they never unreservedly
yield themselves to it. Beware of this.
Humble yourself unto the death. It is in
the death to self that humility is perfected. Be sure that at the root of all
real experience of more grace, of all true
advance in consecration, of all actually
increasing conformity to the likeness of

Jesus, there must be a deadness to self that proves itself to God and men in our dispositions and habits. It is sadly possible to speak of the death-life and the Spirit-walk, while even the tenderest love cannot but see how much there is of self. The death to self has no surer death-mark than a humility which makes itself of no reputation, which empties out itself, and takes the form of a servant. It is possible to speak much and honestly of fellowship with a despised and rejected Jesus, and of bearing His cross, while the meek and lowly, the kind and gentle humility of the Lamb of God is not seen, is scarcely sought. The Lamb of God means two things—meekness and death. Let us seek to receive Him in both forms. In Him they are inseparable : they must be in us too.

What a hopeless task if we had to do the work ! Nature never can overcome nature, not even with the help of grace. Self can never cast out self, even in the regenerate man. Praise God! the work has been done, and finished and perfected for ever. The death of Jesus, once and for ever, is our death to self. And the ascension of Jesus, His entering once and for ever into the Holiest, has given us the Holy Spirit to communicate to us in power, and make our very own, the power of the death-life. As the soul, in the pursuit and practice of humility, follows in the steps of Jesus, its consciousness of the need of something more is awakened, its desire and hope is quickened, its faith is strengthened, and it learns to look up and claim and receive that true fullness of the Spirit of Jesus, which can daily maintain His death to self and sin in its full power, and make humility the all-pervading spirit of our life.[1]

---

[1] See Note C.

"Are ye ignorant that all we who were baptized into Jesus Christ were *baptized into His death?* Reckon yourselves to be *dead unto sin,* but alive unto God in Christ Jesus. Present yourself unto God, as *alive from the dead.*" The whole self-consciousness of the Christian is to be imbued and characterized by the spirit that animated the death of Christ. He has ever to present himself to God as one who has died in Christ, and in Christ is alive from the dead, bearing about in his body the dying of the Lord Jesus. His life ever bears the twofold mark : its roots striking in true humility deep into the grave of Jesus, the death to sin and self; its head lifted up in resurrection power to the heaven where Jesus is.

Believer, claim in faith the death and the life of Jesus as thine. Enter in His grave into the rest from self and its work—the rest of God. With Christ, who committed His spirit into the Father's hands, humble thyself and descend each day into that perfect, helpless dependence upon God. God will raise thee up and exalt thee. Sink every morning in deep, deep nothingness into the grave of Jesus; every day the life of Jesus will be manifest in thee. Let a willing, loving, restful, happy humility be the mark that thou hast indeed claimed thy birthright—the baptism into the death of Christ. "By one offering He hath perfected forever them that are sanctified." The souls that enter into *His* humiliation will find *in Him* the power to see and count self dead, and, as those who have learned and received of Him, to walk with all lowliness and meekness, forbearing one another in love. The death-life is seen in a meekness and lowliness like that of Christ.

XI.

HUMILITY AND HAPPINESS.

" Most gladly therefore will I rather glory in my weaknesses, that the strength of Christ may rest upon me. Wherefore I take pleasure in weaknesses : for when I am weak, then am I strong."—2 Cor. xii. 9. 10.

LEST Paul should exalt himself, by reason of the exceeding greatness of the revelations, a thorn in the flesh was sent him to keep him humble. Paul's first desire was to have it removed, and he besought the Lord thrice that it might depart. The answer came that the trial was a blessing ; that, in the weakness and humiliation it brought, the grace and

(113)

strength of the Lord could be the better manifested. Paul at once entered upon a new stage in his relation to the trial : instead of simply enduring it, *he most gladly gloried* in it ; instead of asking for deliverance, *he took pleasure* in it. He had learned that the place of humiliation is the place of blessing, of power, of joy.

Every Christian virtually passes through these two stages in his pursuit of humility. In the first he fears and flees and seeks deliverance from all that can humble him. He has not yet learned to seek humility at any cost. He has accepted the command to be humble, and seeks to obey it, though only to find how utterly he fails. He prays for humility, at times very earnestly ; but in his secret heart he prays more, if not in word, then in wish, to be kept from the very things that will make him humble. He is not yet so in love with humility as the beauty of the

Lamb of God, and the joy of heaven, that he would sell all to procure it. In his pursuit of it, and his prayer for it, there is still somewhat of a sense of burden and of bondage; to humble himself has not yet become the spontaneous expression of a life and a nature that is essentially humble. It has not yet become his joy and only pleasure. He cannot yet say, "Most gladly do I glory in weakness, I take pleasure in whatever humbles me."

But can we hope to reach the stage in which this will be the case? Undoubtedly. And what will it be that brings us there? *That* which brought Paul there— *a new revelation of the Lord Jesus.* Nothing but the presence of God can reveal and expel self. A clearer insight was to be given to Paul into the deep truth that the presence of Jesus will banish every desire to seek anything in ourselves, and will make us delight in every humiliation that prepares us for His fuller manifestation. Our humiliations lead us, in the experience of the presence and power of Jesus, to choose humility as our highest blessing. Let us try and learn the lessons the story of Paul teaches us.

We may have advanced believers, eminent teachers, men of heavenly experiences, who have not yet fully learned the lesson of perfect humility, gladly glorying in weakness. We see this in Paul. The danger of exalting himself was coming very near. He knew not yet perfectly what it was to be nothing; to die, that Christ alone might live in him; to take pleasure in all that brought him low. It appears as if this were the highest lesson that he had to learn, full conformity to his lord in that self-emptying where he gloried in weakness that God might be all.

The highest lesson a believer has to

learn is humility. Oh that every Christian who seeks to advance in holiness may remember this well! There may be intense consecration, and fervent zeal and heavenly experience, and yet, if it is not prevented by very special dealings of the Lord, there may be an unconscious self-exaltation with it all. Let us learn the lesson,—the highest holiness is the deepest humility ; and let us remember that it comes not of itself, but only as it is made a matter of special dealing on the part of our faithful Lord and His faithful servant.

Let us look at our lives in the light of this experience, and see whether we gladly glory in weakness, whether we take pleasure, as Paul did, in injuries, in necessities, in distresses. Yes, let us ask whether we have learned to regard a reproof, just or unjust, a reproach from friend or enemy, an injury, or trouble, or difficulty into which others bring us, as above all an opportunity of proving how Jesus is all to us, how our own pleasure or honor are nothing, and how humiliation is in very truth what we take pleasure in. It is indeed blessed, the deep happiness of heaven, to be so free from self that whatever is said of us or done to us is lost and swallowed up in the thought that Jesus is all.

Let us trust Him who took charge of Paul to take charge of us too. Paul needed special discipline, and with it special instruction, to learn, what was more precious than even the unutterable things he had heard in heaven—what it is to glory in weakness and lowliness. We need it, too, oh so much. He who cared for him will care for us too. The school in which Jesus taught Paul is our school too. He watches over us with a jealous loving care, "lest we exalt our-

selves." When we are doing so, He seeks
to discover to us the evil, and deliver us
from it. In trial and weakness and
trouble He seeks to bring us low, until
we so learn that His grace is all, as to
take pleasure in the very thing that
brings us and keeps us low. His strength
made perfect in our weakness, His presence filling and satisfying our emptiness,
becomes the secret of a humility that
need never fail. It can, as Paul, in full
sight of what God works in us and
through us, ever say, " In nothing was I
behind the chiefest apostles, *though I am
nothing.*" His humiliations had led him
to true humility, with its wonderful gladness and glorying and pleasure in all that
humbles.

"Most gladly will I glory in my weaknesses, that the power of Christ may rest
upon me ; wherefore I take pleasure in
weaknesses." The humble man has

learned the secret of abiding gladness.
The weaker he feels, the lower he sinks,
the greater his humiliations appear, the
more the power and the presence of Christ
are his portion, until, as he says, "I am
nothing," the word of his Lord brings
ever deeper joy : "My grace is sufficient
for thee."

I feel as if I must once again gather
up all in the two lessons : the danger of
pride is greater and nearer than we think,
and the grace for humility too.

*The danger of pride is greater and
nearer than we think,* and that especially
at the time of our highest experiences.
The preacher of spiritual truth with an
admiring congregation hanging on his
lips, the gifted speaker on a Holiness
platform expounding the secrets of the
heavenly life, the Christian giving testimony to a blessed experience, the evan-
gelist moving on as in triumph, and

made a blessing to rejoicing multitudes, —no man knows the hidden, the unconscious danger to which these are exposed. Paul was in danger without knowing it : what Jesus did for him is written for our admonition, that we may know our danger and know our only safety. If ever it has been said of a teacher or professor of holiness,—he is so full of self; or, he does not practice what he preaches ; or, his blessing has not made him humbler or gentler, — let it be said no more. Jesus, in whom we trust, can make us humble.

Yes, the grace for humility is greater and nearer, too, than we think. The humility of Jesus is our salvation : Jesus Himself is our humility. Our humility is His care and His work. His grace is sufficient for us to meet the temptation of pride too. His strength will be perfected in our weakness. Let us choose to be weak, to be low, to be nothing. Let humility be to us joy and gladness. Let us gladly glory and take pleasure in weakness, in all that can humble us and keep us low; the power of Christ will rest upon us. Christ humbled Himself, therefore God exalted Him. Christ will humble us, and keep us humble; let us heartily consent, let us trustfully and joyfully accept all that humbles; the power of Christ will rest upon us. We shall find that the deepest humility is the secret of the truest happiness, of a joy that nothing can destroy.

XII.

HUMILITY AND EXALTATION.

"He that humbleth himself shall be exalted."
—LUKE xiv. 11, xviii. 13.

"God giveth grace to the humble. Humble yourself in the sight of the Lord, and He shall exalt you."—JAS. iv. 10.

"Humble yourselves therefore under the mighty hand of God, that He may exalt you in due time."—1 PET. v. 6.

JUST yesterday I was asked the question, How am I to conquer this pride? The answer was simple. Two things are needed. Do what God says is your work: humble yourself. Trust Him to do what He says is His work: He will exalt you

The command is clear: humble your-

self. That does not mean that it is your
work to conquer and cast out the pride
of your nature, and to form within yourself the lowliness of the holy Jesus. No,
this is God's work; the very essence of
that exaltation, wherein He lifts you up
into the real likeness of the beloved Son.
What the command does mean is this:
take every opportunity of humbling yourself before God and man. In the faith
of the grace that is already working in
you; in the assurance of the more grace
for victory that is coming; up to the light
that conscience each time flashes upon
the pride of the heart and its workings;
notwithstanding all there may be of failure and falling, stand persistently as under
the unchanging command: humble yourself. Accept with gratitude everything
that God allows from within or without,
from friend or enemy, in nature or in
grace, to remind you of your need of

humbling, and to help you to it. Reckon humility to be indeed the mother-virtue, your very first duty before God, the one perpetual safeguard of the soul, and set your heart upon it as the source of all blessing. The promise is divine and sure : He that humbleth himself shall be exalted. See that you do the one thing God asks : humble yourself. God will see that He does the one thing He has promised. He will give more grace; He will exalt you in due time.

All God's dealings with man are characterized by two stages. There is the time of preparation, when command and promise, with the mingled experience of effort and impotence, of failure and partial success, with the holy expectancy of something better which these waken, train and discipline men for a higher stage. Then comes the time of fulfillment, when faith inherits the promise, and enjoys what it had so often struggled for in vain. This law holds good in every part of the Christian life, and in the pursuit of every separate virtue. And that because it is grounded in the very nature of things. In all that concerns our redemption, God must needs take the initiative. When that has been done, man's turn comes. In the effort after obedience and attainment, he must learn to know his impotence, in self-despair to die to himself, and so be fitted voluntarily and intelligently to receive from God the end, the completion of that of which he had accepted the beginning in ignorance. So, God who had been the Beginning, ere man rightly knew Him, or fully understood what His purpose was, is longed for and welcomed as the End, as the All in All.

It is even thus, too, in the pursuit of humility. To every Christian the command comes from the throne of God Himself : humble yourself. The earnest attempt to listen and obey will be rewarded—yes, rewarded—with the painful discovery of two things. The one, what depth of pride, that is of unwillingness to count oneself and to be counted nothing, to submit absolutely to God, there was, that one never knew. The other, what utter impotence there is in all our efforts, and in all our prayers too for God's help, to destroy the hideous monster. Blessed the man who now learns to put his hope in God, and to persevere, notwithstanding all the power of pride within him, in acts of humiliation before God and men. We know the law of human nature: acts produce habits, habits breed dispositions, dispositions form the will, and the rightly-formed will is character. It is no otherwise in the work of grace. As acts, persistently repeated, beget habits and dispositions, and these strengthen the will, He who works both to will and to do comes with His mighty power and Spirit; and the humbling of the proud heart with which the penitent saint cast himself so often before God, is rewarded with the "more grace" of the humble heart, in which the Spirit of Jesus has conquered, and brought the new nature to its maturity, and He the meek and lowly One now dwells for ever.

Humble yourselves in the sight of the Lord, and He will exalt you. And wherein does the exaltation consist? The highest glory of the creature is in being only a vessel, to receive and enjoy and show forth the glory of God. It can do this only as it is willing to be nothing in itself, that God may be all. Water always fills first the lowest places. The lower, the emptier a man lies before God, the speedier and the fuller will be the inflow

of the divine glory. The exaltation God
promises is not, cannot be, any external
thing apart from Himself: all that He
has to give or can give is only more of
Himself, Himself to take more complete
possession. The exaltation is not, like
an earthly prize, something arbitrary, in
no necessary connection with the conduct
to be rewarded. No, but it is in its very
nature the effect and result of the humbling of ourselves. It is nothing but the
gift of such a divine indwelling humility,
such a conformity to and possession of
the humility of the Lamb of God, as fits
us for receiving fully the indwelling of
God.

He that humbleth himself shall be exalted. Of the truth of these words Jesus
Himself is the proof; of the certainty of
their fulfillment to us He is the pledge.
Let us take His yoke upon us and learn
of Him, for He is meek and lowly of

heart. If we are but willing to stoop to Him, as He has stooped to us, He will yet stoop to each one of us again, and we shall find ourselves not unequally yoked with Him. As we enter deeper into the fellowship of His humiliation, and either humble ourselves or bear the humbling of men, we can count upon it that the Spirit of His exaltation, "the Spirit of God and of glory," will rest upon us. The presence and the power of the glorified Christ will come to them that are of an humble spirit. When God can again have His rightful place in us, He will lift us up. Make His glory thy care in humbling thyself; He will make thy glory His care in perfecting thy humility, and breathing into thee, as thy abiding life, the very Spirit of His Son. As the all-pervading life of God possesses thee, there will be nothing so natural, and nothing so sweet, as to be nothing, with

not a thought or wish for self, because
all is occupied with Him who filleth all,
"Most gladly will I glory in my weakness, that the strength of Christ may rest
upon me."

Brother, have we not here the reason
that our consecration and our faith have
availed so little in the pursuit of holiness? It was by self and its strength that
the work was done under the name of
faith ; it was for self and its happiness
that God was called in ; it was, unconsciously, but still truly, in self and its
holiness that the soul rejoiced. We never
knew that humility, absolute, abiding,
Christlike humility and self-effacement,
pervading and marking our whole life
with God and man, was the most essential element of the life of the holiness we
sought for.

It is only in the possession of God that
I lose myself. As it is in the height and

breadth and glory of the sunshine that
the littleness of the mote playing in its
beams is seen, even so humility is the
taking our place in God's presence to be
nothing but a mote dwelling in the sun-
light of His love.

" How great is God ! how small am I !
  Lost, swallowed up in Love's immensity !
     God only there, not I."

May God teach us to believe that to be
humble, to be nothing in His presence, is
the highest attainment, and the fullest
blessing, of the Christian life. He speaks
to us : " I dwell in the high and holy
place, and with him that is of a contrite
and humble spirit." Be this our portion !

" Oh, to be emptier, lowlier,
  Mean, unnoticed, and unknown,
And to God a vessel holier,
  Filled with Christ, and Christ alone !"

NOTES

NOTE A.—"All this to make it known through the region of eternity that *pride* can degrade the highest angels into devils, and humility raise fallen flesh and blood to the thrones of angels. Thus, this is the great end of God raising a new creation out of a fallen kingdom of angels; for this end it stands in its state of war betwixt the fire and pride of fallen angels, and the humility of the Lamb of God, that the last trumpet may sound the great truth through the depths of eternity, that evil can have no beginning but from pride, and no end but from humility. The truth is this : Pride must die in you, or nothing of heaven can live in you. Under the banner of the truth, give yourself up to the meek and humble spirit of the holy Jesus. Humility must sow the seed, or there can be no reaping in heaven. Look not at pride only as an unbecoming temper, nor at humility only as a decent virtue : for the one is death, and the other is life ; the one is all hell, the other is all heaven. So much as you have of pride within you, you have of the fallen angel alive in you ; so much as you have of true humility, so much you have of the Lamb of God within you. Could you see what every stirring of pride does to your soul, you would beg of everything you meet to tear the viper from you, though with the loss of a hand or an eye. Could you see what a sweet, divine, transforming power there is in humility, how it expels the poison of your nature, and makes room for the Spirit of God to live in you, you would rather wish to be the foot-stool of all the world than want the smallest degree of it."—*Spirit of Prayer*, Pt. II., p. 73, Edition of Moreton, Canterbury, 1893.

NOTE B.—"We need to know two things : 1. That our salvation consists wholly in being saved from *ourselves,* or that which we are by nature ; 2. That in the whole nature of things nothing could be this salvation or saviour to us but such a humility of God as is beyond all expression. Hence the first unalterable term of the Saviour to fallen man : Except a man denies *himself*, he cannot be My disciple. Self is the whole evil of fallen nature : self-denial is our capacity of being saved ; humility is our saviour. . . . . *Self* is the root, the branches, the tree, of all the evil of our fallen state. All the evils of fallen angels and men have their birth in the pride of self. On the other hand, all the virtues of the heavenly life are the virtues of humility. It is humility alone that makes the unpassable gulf between heaven and hell. What is then, or in what lies, the great struggle for eternal life ? It all lies in the strife between *pride* and *humility :* pride and humility are the two master powers, the two kingdoms in strife for the eternal possession of man. There never was, nor ever will be, but one humility, and that is the one humility of Christ. Pride and self have the all of man, till man has his all from Christ. He therefore only fights the good fight whose strife is that the self-idolatrous nature which he hath from Adam may be brought to death by the supernatural humility of Christ brought to life in him."—W. Law, *Address to the Clergy,* p. 52. [I hope that this book of Law on the Holy Spirit may be issued by my publisher in the course of the year.]

NOTE C.—" To die to self, or come from under its power, is not, cannot be done, by any active resistance we can make to it by the powers of nature. The one true way of dying to self is the way of *patience, meekness, humility, and resignation to God.* This is the truth and perfection of dying to self. . . . . For if I ask you what the Lamb of God means, must you not tell me that it is and means the perfection of *patience, meekness, humility, and resignation to God?* Must you not therefore say that a desire and faith of these virtues is an application to Christ, is a giving up yourself to Him and the perfection of faith in Him? And then, because this inclination of your heart to sink down in *patience, meekness, humility, and resignation to God,* is truly giving up all that you are and all that you have from fallen Adam, it is perfectly leaving all you have to follow Christ; it is your highest act of faith in Him. Christ is nowhere but in these virtues ; when they are there, He is in His own kingdom. Let this be the Christ you follow.

" The Spirit of divine love can have no birth in any fallen creature, till it wills and chooses to be dead to all self, in a *patient, humble resignation* to the power and mercy of God.

"I seek for all my salvation through the merits and mediation of the *meek, humble, patient, suffering Lamb of God*, who alone hath power to bring forth the blessed birth of these heavenly virtues in my soul. There is no possibility of salvation but in and by the birth of the *meek, humble, patient, resigned Lamb of God* in our souls. When the Lamb of God hath brought forth a real birth of His own *meekness, humility, and full resignation to God* in our souls, then it is the birthday of the Spirit of love in our souls, which, whenever we attain, will feast our souls with such peace and joy in God as will blot out the remembrance of everything that we called peace or joy before.

" This way to God is infallible. This infallibility is grounded in the twofold character of our Saviour : 1. As He is the Lamb of God, a principle of all *meek-*

ness and humility in the soul; 2. As he is the Light of heaven, and blesses eternal nature, and turns it into a kingdom of heaven,—when we are willing to get rest to our souls in meek, humble resignation to God, then it is that He, as the Light of God and heaven, joyfully breaks in upon us, turns our darkness into light, and begins that kingdom of God and of love within us, which will never have an end."—See *Wholly for God*, pp. 84–102. [The whole passage deserves careful study, showing most remarkably how the continual sinking down in humility before God is, from man's side, the only way to die to self.]

NOTE D.—*A Secret of Secrets: Humility the Soul of True Prayer.*—Till the spirit of the heart be renewed, till it is emptied of all earthly desires, and stands in an habitual hunger and thirst after God, which is the true spirit of prayer; till then, all our prayer will be, more or less, but too much like lessons given to scholars; and we shall mostly say them, only because we dare not neglect them. But be not discouraged; take the following advice, and then you may go to church without any danger of mere lip-labor or hypocrisy, although there should be a hymn or a prayer, whose language is higher than that of your heart. Do this: go to the church as the publican went to the temple; stand inwardly in the spirit of your mind in that form which he outwardly expressed, when he cast down his eyes, and could only say, "God be merciful to me, a sinner." Stand unchangeably, at least in your desire, in this form or state of heart; it will sanctify every petition that comes out of your mouth; and when anything is read or sung or prayed, that is more exalted than your heart is, if you make this an occasion of further sinking down in the spirit of the publican, you will then be helped, and highly blessed, by those prayers and praises which seem only to belong to a heart better than yours.

This, my friend, is a secret of secrets; it will help you to reap where you have not sown, and be a continual source of grace in your soul; for everything that inwardly stirs in you, or outwardly happens to you, becomes a real good to you, if its finds or excites in you *this humble state of mind.* For nothing is in vain, or without profit to *the humble soul;* it stands always in a state of divine growth ; everything that falls upon it is like a dew of heaven to it. Shut up yourself, therefore, in this *form of Humility;* all good is enclosed in it ; it is a water of heaven, that turns the fire of the fallen soul into the meekness of the divine life, and creates that oil, out of which the love to God and man gets its flame. Be enclosed, therefore, always in it ; let it be as a garment wherewith you are always covered, and a girdle with which you are girt ; breathe nothing but in and from its spirit ; see nothing but with its eyes ; hear nothing but with its ears. And then, whether you are in the church or out of the church, hearing the praises of God or receiving wrongs from men and the world, all will be edification, and everything will help forward your growth in the life of God.— *The Spirit of Prayer*, Pt. II., p. 121.

A Prayer for Humility.

I will here give you an infallible touchstone, that will try all to the truth. It is this : retire from the world and all conversation, only for one month ; neither write, nor read, nor debate anything with yourself; stop all the former workings of your heart and mind: and, with all the strength of your heart, stand all this month, as continually as you can, in the following form of prayer to God. Offer it frequently on your knees; but whether sitting, walking, or standing, be always inwardly longing, and earnestly praying this one prayer to God: "That of His great goodness He would make known to you, and take from your heart, *every kind and form and degree of Pride*, whether it be from evil spirits, or your own corrupt nature; and that He would awaken in you the *deepest depth and truth of that Humility*, which can make you capable of His light and Holy Spirit." Reject every thought, but that of waiting and praying in this matter from the bottom of your heart, with such truth and earnestness, as people in torment wish to pray and be delivered from it. . . . . If you can and will give yourselves up in truth and sincerity to this spirit of prayer, I will venture to affirm that, if you had twice as many evil spirits in you as Mary Magdalene had, they will all be cast out of you, and you will be forced with her to weep tears of love at the feet of the holy Jesus.—*Ibid.*, p. 124.

By Rev. A. J. Gordon, D.D.

The Ministry of the Spirit. Introduction by Rev.
F. B. Meyer, B.A. 12mo, cloth, gilt top...........$1.00
CHEAP EDITION, 18mo, cloth, net, 25c.; by post. net, .30

How Christ Came to Church: The Pastor's Dream.
A Spiritual Autobiography. With the life-story and the
dream as interpreting the man, by Rev. A. T. Pierson,
D.D. With portrait. 8vo, cloth, gilt top......... .75
CHEAP EDITION, 18mo, cloth, net, 25c.; by post, net, .30

In Christ; or, the Believer's Union with his Lord.
12mo, cloth, gilt top, $1.00; paper................net, .35
POCKET EDITION, uniform with "A Gift of Love."
Long 18mo, cloth.... .... 1.00
CHEAP EDITION, 18mo, cloth, net, 25c.; by post, net, .30

The Holy Spirit in Missions. 12mo, cloth, gilt
top... 1.25

Grace and Glory. Sermons for the Life that Now is
and That which is to Come. 12mo, cloth, gilt top 1.50
Paper...net, .50

Ecce Venit; or, Behold He Cometh. 12mo, cloth,
gilt top, $1.25; paper ....net .50

The Ministry of Healing; or, Miracles of Cures in
all ages. With History of the Doctrine from the Earli-
est Times. 12mo, cloth, gilt top, $1.25; paper, net, .50

The Two-Fold Life; or, Christ's Work for Us, and
Christ's Work in Us. 12mo, cloth, gilt top.... .... 1.25
Paper...net, .50

Risen with Christ; or, the Resurrection of Christ
and of the Believer. 16mo, boards................ .30

The First Thing in the World; or, the Primacy of
Faith. 16mo, Popular Vellum Series.............. .20
CHEAP EDITION, net, 10c.; per doz..............net, 1.00

The Coronation Hymnal. 400 Hymns, with Music.
By Rev. Drs. A. J. Gordon and A. T. Pierson. 4to,
half-cloth, red edges, net, 60c.; cloth, red edges, net, .75

Two editions: An edition for general use, and a Bap-
tist edition. Send for specimen pages.

By Rev. F. B. Meyer

The Shepherd Psalm. Illustrated. Printed in two colors. 12mo, cloth, gilt top, boxed, $1.25; full gilt, $1.50.

The Bells of Is. Echoes from my early pastorates. With portrait. 12mo, cloth, 75 c.

Prayers for Heart and Home. 8vo, flex. cloth, 75 c.

Paul : a Servant of Jesus Christ. 12mo, cloth, $1.00.

Old Testament Heroes. 8 vols., 12mo, cloth, each, $1.00 ; the set, boxed, $8.00.

Abraham.	Elijah.	Jeremiah.	Joshua.
David.	Israel.	Joseph.	Moses.

The Expository Series. 12mo, cloth, each $1.00 ; the set, boxed, $4.00.

Tried by Fire.	The Way Into the Holiest.
Christ in Isaiah.	The Life and Light of Men.

The Christian Life Series. 18mo, cloth, each, 30 c.

The Shepherd Psalm	Through Fire and Flood.
Christian Living.	The Glorious Lord.
The Present Tenses	Calvary to Pentecost.
The Future Tenses	Key Words to the Inner Life.

*** The first four also issued in flexible, decorated cloth, 16mo, each, 50 c. ; the set, boxed, $2.00.

Addresses. 12mo, paper, each, 15 c.; cloth, each, net, 30c.

Meet for the Master's Use	A Castaway
The Secret of Guidance	Light on Life's Duties

Saved and Kept. Long 16mo, cloth, 50 c.

Cheer for Life's Pilgrimage. Long 16mo, cloth, 50 c.

Peace, Perfect Peace. 18mo, cloth, 25 c.

The Psalms. Notes and Readings. 18mo, cloth, 60 c.

Envelope Series of Booklets. Packets Nos. 1 and 2, each containing 12 Tracts, assorted, net, 20 c.

Choice Extracts. 24mo, paper, each, 5 c.; per doz. net, 35 c.; 16mo, paper, 15 c.